There's A Hole In My Sidewalk

The Romance of Self-Discovery

by Portia Nelson

BEYOND WORDS PUBLISHING, INC.

Beyond Words Publishing, Inc.
4443 NE Airport Rd.
Hillsboro, OR 97124
(503) 693-8700 tel
(503) 693-6888 fax

Typesetting: The TypeSmith
Design: Soga Design/ Principia Graphica

Previously published under
ISBN: 0-9621159-0-8 & 0-445-03199-9
Printed in Canada
Distributed by Publishers Group West

Library of Congress Cataloging-in-Publication Data

Nelson, Portia.
    There's a hole in my sidewalk : the romance of self-discovery / by
Portia Nelson.
        p.   cm.
    Originally published : Los Angeles : Popular Library, 1977.
    ISBN 0-941831-87-6 : $7.95
    1. Self-realization.   2. Self-perception.   3. Maturation
(Psychology)   I. Title.
BF637.S4N45   1993
158'.1—dc20   93-18380
                                                        CIP

• • • • • • • • • • • •

I am part of all
that I have met."
—Tennyson

To all of you,
whoever you are,
I humbly dedicate
this book.

• • • • • • • • • • • •

PERSONAL NOTE

I choose to call these thoughts "pieces"... pieces of me. These pieces have had a bit of trouble finding a comfortable concept that would knit them into one book ... just as I have had difficulty molding a multi-faceted misfit into one person.

More than anything, they are evidence, to me, that here in the middle of my life I have finally gained a small pin-point of self-awareness ... false images stripped away ... "through a glass darkly, but, now ... face to face." No hiding, anymore, behind innocence and ignorance.

It isn't necessarily easier now ... but I have a self that I trust and the feelings and the experiences are mine ... not what I *should* feel ... not what I was taught to feel and not something someone else felt that I admired and imitated. Knowing one's own feelings and being able to trust them is the difference between existing and living. So, that's what I have here, I guess ... living and loving experiences ... pieces of my small universe that can, I hope, be recognized by yours.

CONTENTS

A story of
Me in You
and
You in Me
in
Five Short Chapters

PROLOGUE

My life has been a series
of wonderful experiences.
It's a pity I wasn't there
for most of them.

AUTOBIOGRAPHY IN FIVE SHORT CHAPTERS

CHAPTER ONE

I walk down the street.
>There is a deep hole in the sidewalk.
>I fall in.
>I am lost . . . . I am helpless.
>>It isn't my fault.
It takes forever to find a way out.

CHAPTER TWO

I walk down the same street.
>There is a deep hole in the sidewalk.
>I pretend I don't see it.
>I fall in again.
I can't believe I am in this same place.
>>But, it isn't my fault.
It still takes a long time to get out.

CHAPTER THREE

I walk down the same street.
>   There is a deep hole in the sidewalk.
>   I *see* it is there.
>   I still fall in . . . it's a habit . . . but,
>   my eyes are open.
>   I know where I am.

It is *my* fault.
I get out immediately.

CHAPTER FOUR

I walk down the same street.
>   There is a deep hole in the sidewalk.
>   I walk around it.

CHAPTER FIVE

I walk down another street.

CHAPTER ONE

I don't know what I want sometimes,
But I know
that I want to know
what I want.
I know that once I know what I want
I will be able to get it.
Of course, I may not want what I get
when I get it . . . .
But, at least
I'll know I don't want that!
Then, I can move on to something else
I don't know if I want.
That's progress!

You say you love me for who I am . . . .
But . . .
who you think I am
is not *who* I am.

Therefore,
it's hard for me to be who I am
when we're together . . .

because . . .
I think I have to be
who you think I am.

Of course,
I don't know exactly who it is
you think I am . . .
I just know it isn't who I am.

Who am I?
Well . . .
Who I am is something I recognize
when someone tells me
who I am *not*.
At least, I *think* that's *not* who I am.
Maybe who I am *not*
is who I *am*!
If that's who I am . . . MY GAWD . . .
you really love me.

I used to suffer a great deal
thinking I was the only one
in the world
so lonely
and troubled.

Then, I opened the door to myself
and discovered there were
millions
of people
just like me.

It isn't lonely anymore . . .
but it's miserable to be
so ordinary.

I know why we are friends.
It's because I don't always
approve of you.

You don't think you deserve approval.
So . . . if I gave it to you,
you would not
approve of me
and I would lose your trust.

Friendship is based on trust
and I want you
to trust me
because I need your approval.

However, if I get your approval,
I will not trust you
because I don't think I deserve approval
either.

I know why we are friends.

You want to please me . . . and,

I want to please you . . .

> so please make the decision
> about where we are going tonight.

If I make the decision . . .
> and then *you* don't like it,
> you'll be mad at me
> and I'll be miserable all evening
> because I haven't pleased you.

Now . . . if *you* try to please me . . .
> and *you* make the decision,
> and *I* don't like it
> when we get there . . .
> at least *you* will be pleased.

If I am unhappy with where we are,
　　　or what we are doing,
　　　that's alright. . . .

because it won't be my decision
that will have made you unhappy.
　　　It will be yours.
　　　Therefore,
　　　it will be *your* fault!
　　　　　That will please me.

You say you will never leave me
        because I understand you.
And I love being thought of
        as "understanding."

But, I also understand
        that by being so understanding,
        you automatically
        have the freedom
        to do as you please . . .
        because . . .
if I am not understanding,
        you will leave me.

I think that what I really
        have to understand is this:
In order to be so understanding all the time
        (so that you will not leave me),
        I have to leave myself.

If I am not myself
       when I am being so understanding,
       who the hell is it
       you will never leave?

Better I should not be so understanding
       so there's somebody
       you can leave.

You have made a fool of me!

I know that I am not the most beautiful,
the most talented, the most intelligent
person in the world . . .
but I liked you . . .
and I wanted you
to think I was.
So . . . I tried to be beautiful
talented and intelligent
for you.

However,
since I succeeded
in making you believe it,
naturally,
I immediately
lost respect for you
for not seeing
that I had fooled you.

Now . . .
I am intelligent enough,
beautiful enough and
talented enough

not to be associated with fools . . .
and I am incensed that I didn't see
        how foolish you were
                at once.

But . . .
        I liked you then . . . and . . .
it drove me to make you believe
        what I wanted you to believe . . . .

Except . . .
        I was so convincing,
        I began to believe it myself!

Now . . .
        anybody who believes
        things like that about me
                is a fool.

That makes me a fool!

And if it weren't for you
        believing what I wanted you to believe,
        I wouldn't know that.

I hate you for making a fool of me!

Will you please stop trying to
finish my sentences before I do?

It's humiliating!

After all . . . it's my sentence!
Let me show it off!

I know you are really trying to let me know
how sensitive and smart you are . . .
and how deeply you understand me . . . .

But . . . if you are that smart . . .
please let me think that
I am smarter than you
by not impressing me with
how smart you are
in the middle of my sentences!

Of course,
       if I am smart enough
       to be aware of
       what you are up to . . .

Then,
       I should be smart enough to know
       it doesn't matter what you do
       in the middle of my sentences.

Maybe I'm not so smart!

Now, that *is* humiliating!

I want you to love me . . .
>   but I am aware
>   that you only love
>   what you cannot get.
>   So, I can't let you know
>   that I am interested
>   or you won't love me back.

Now . . .
>   I hate games
>   and dishonesty
>   more than anything.

Therefore . . .
>   if I love you enough
>   to be dishonest . . .
>   to play a game
>   in order to keep you interested,
>   I will hate myself.
>   If I hate myself,
>   eventually,
>   I will crack up!

If I crack up . . .
        at least,
        you won't be able to get me . . .
                because I won't care . . .
                or be aware
                that you even exist . . .
        and then,
        maybe you will love me.

Jesus! There's got to be a simpler way!

You are strong . . . vital . . .
>very much in control of yourself.
I admire that!
I know you can help me . . .
>and I need help.

But,

>if I allow you to help me,
>I will have to trust you enough
>to give up my own self control.

If I give that up,
>I will begin to feel powerless . . .
>without identity . . .
>like a nobody!

How dare you help me to be a nobody!

I cannot seem to leave you . . .
though often,
I think I should because
even though I care . . .
I am not in love with you.
But I am in love with the fact
that you are in love with me.
It makes me think very well of myself.
When I think well of myself,
I am very nice . . .
and very creative.
That makes me feel worthwhile and then
I love myself.
The more I love myself . . .
the more you love me.
No wonder I can't leave.
I wouldn't know
I loved myself . . .
without you.

I would like to be one . . .
A one not worried about being two!
I am more one
        when we are three.
When we are two,
        I become zero.
I become zero because
I am afraid you will see
        that I am not one.
When we are three, I am comfortable . . .
It doesn't matter if I am not one
        since I seem to become one
        simply because
        there are two being two
        and letting me be one.
Therefore, I am not zero . . . I can't be . . .
Two from three is always one.
So, I am more one when we are three . . .
        as long as I don't worry about
                being two.

In the beginning,
        everywhere I went,
        I didn't always go along.
I didn't know it then,
        but I was afraid I'd meet myself.
When we finally met,
I wasn't who I expected I'd be . . .
        but, oh, it was a relief
        to have someone to be with . . .
                at last.

CHAPTER TWO

I am a hopeless romantic
      who does not believe
      love solves everything.
Still, I weep for the loss
      of illusion . . .
      knowing full well
      that reality
      is unbearable . . .
without a few gilded window frames
      to see through.

How brazen you are!

You lean across the table . . .
        slender hands
        cupping your face . . .

and stare arrow-straight
        into my eyes . . .
        no blinking at all.

You know you are making a frame

for a remarkably beautiful face.

I stare back . . .
        not out of desire
        or challenge . . .

        but as my only defense
        against your discovering

how deeply I am immersed in pleasure.

I hope that what you are after
is an exchange . . .
                    not
            a reaction.

One step forward
        into the bright of loving.
Yet, I fear the bright will not last.
        . . . so, one step back.
Still, I fear more,
        the dark of not loving at all.
Well then . . .
        may I take a giant step?
        May I?
I have already answered.
        Shall we dance?

I know who you are.

You are so much of me
      that if I don't love you
      I won't exist.

And I'm selfish.
      I don't want to miss anything.

Two days ago
I never would have believed
I would spring from my bed
        at the first glimmer
                of sunlight . . .
and drive all over town
        looking for
        blue Volkswagens!

Dear one . . .

Kind one . . .

> lend me your dreams
> for a while.

Cover me
> with the sweet sleep
> of your innocence,
and wake me
> with the crystal sunshine
> of your hope.

Light my darkness with fireflies
> and build me air castles
> to house
> the velvet summers
> of love.

Stay with me,
        dear one . . .
stay with me long enough
        to let me hear again,
        that far away music
        of yesterday . . .
                when I was young.

Your hair is like a monk's cap
            made of wheat.

It often slips down over your eyes
            so I can't see if you are
            hiding from me
            or spying on me.

Sometimes,
            I reach out . . .
            as an artist might . . .
and make a gentle brush stroke
            on the canvas of your brow
            to change the shape of your cap.

As much as I love it,
I cannot bear to talk to you
            without watching your eyes.

Besides,
> there is such selfish pleasure
> in the act of touching,
> lightly . . .
> hardly at all . . .

making a graceful arc there
and seeing you smile . . .
> as if your hair were attached
> to the corners of your mouth.

There is so much about me that I don't know
until I talk to you.

That first day . . .
          as you turned to leave . . .
          we touched . . .
and, like magnets, we clung to one another
          for a long time.
          Nothing more.
Yet. . .in that rare moment of holding you
I experienced what I have come to value most . . .
          the ecstasy
          of
          not doing anything
          about it.

How wise of you to wait . . .
to fill the shy, awkward spaces
        with white wine
        and cushioned conversation.
I am aware that you are
        allowing me time
        to become accustomed
to the cities of your smile . . .
and to window shop your eyes . . .
        until, at last,
        I am so full of you,
that I no longer blush
        on my way into your arms.

Water, Air, Earth, Fire.

Mix together slowly,
        with ceiling seagulls
        and pear wine.

Stir until the perfect blend . . .

Cool for a moment . . . then,
        place in the fruitful womb
        of love
        to be born again
        into a circle of light . . .

an enchanted world where only believers
        are allowed to enter.

I can feel my fears beginning
                to settle inside me . . .
                like sleepy kittens
                upon the hearth
Shshshsh . . . tip toe . . .
Don't slam doors in my mind . . .
                not now.
Let the kittens sleep a little while
                please . . .
The fire will die soon enough, anyway . . .
And now, while the world is warm . . .
                hold me.

I think I just fell into a hole
in the sidewalk.

I have said, "I love you" . . .
        before you,
        and meant it.

Yet,
I would have to admit . . .
        that laid on the scales,
        the pain of loving
        has often outweighed the joy.

But, it never ceases to amaze me
        that I never died of love.

Looking back . . .
        knowing I survived . . .
        pain has become my faith.

Though I am fragile . . .
        it is my strength.

So, I warn you . . .
        I will not die of you.

I know that pain and joy
          cannot be separated . . .
          and, like tomorrow and today
          they become one another.

And so, I remember those
          before you,
and rejoice that I said,
          "I love you"
          before you . . .

because,
it will help me not to die of you . . .
          like I didn't
          before you.

I am always a grumbling sleepwalker
in the mornings.

Do you realize . . .
for three days in a row
I have laughed
at least ten times
before coffee?

It's a dreary day . . . .
Let's just stay inside.
We can pretend that
        Kisses are brushes
        and that we are
        each other's canvases.
We won't need a northern light . . .
        or any light at all,
        for that matter . . . .
And who cares if we ever finish
        the picture, anyway.

Sorry I didn't answer.
I was listening
        to what you weren't saying.

You are the oldest young person
I have ever known.
It makes me feel younger than you are.
That's a neat trick!

I am so free with you,
I never wish to be
    free of you.

The beautiful togetherness
          of our silence
               makes me wonder
why we ever bothered
               to speak at all.

I didn't really
        leave my heart
        in San Francisco . . .
although I said I did . . . .
But, I certainly
        let it out
        into the fresh
            morning air
and ran it up and down
        a few hills.
I did let it rest
        in the smile
of a beautiful stranger
        for a few days . . . .
But then,
        I snatched it away
        and brought it home
            to you . . .
as I knew I would
        before I went away
        to be mad at you.

I think I love you most
in those early hours
just before sunrise
When,
spent with loving
and lost in dreaming,
You reach out,
like the morning glory vine,
and wind about,
braiding limb to limb,
binding me to you
with the tender quiet
of us.
Desire is buried in slumber . . .
and,
asking nothing . . .
giving all . . .
You bend to touch me
through a thousand years of knowing
. . . without knowing.
But I know.
I'm glad I'm a light sleeper.

When I listen
        to your feelings,
        and can feel
        your listenings . . .
Only then
        can I expect you
        to hear me.

We are not "in love"...
but, we are love.
I'm glad.
It lasts longer.

My longing is burning a hole
        in my patience . . . .
        Time is spinning away.
What good is sleep
        when an eternity
        is rushing by
        that I could be kissing you?

Damn it!
Will you please wake up?
I think I'll turn over . . .
        a little bump
        never hurt anybody!
"Hey! . . . awake so early?
        I love you."

Please understand . . .
There are days I must leave you . . .
        in order to be closer to you.
Up close, I cannot search out
        those fragments of you
        that your image of yourself
        hides from me.
At a distance . . .
        uncluttered by sensation . . .
        I can really see you, freely . . .
        and discover pieces of myself,
        as well.
And then, we come home together . . .
        to love you all the more.

You said you didn't love me
            this morning.
I didn't believe you.
I knew you just hated yourself.
            That's alright.
I don't love you either . . .
            today.

Please . . .
don't extract promises from me
that must race quickly
           from the present
           into the past
casting dark shadows on the future.
Now . . . today . . . is all
           we can be certain of
           and love
           is something better
than a collection of pretty vows
to cling to on a rainy day.
What we already are
           is what we will be
                     together.
           Isn't that enough?

Stop looking at me like that!
Can't you see how much
        I need you to believe
        what I am saying
so that I can believe it
        myself?

I would give you everything . . .
                if I could . . . but,
the only gift worth giving
                is freedom . . .
the freedom to grow . . .
                away from me,
                if necessary.
Of course, one can't give freedom,
but, at least I know that.
Maybe that's the gift then . . .
                the knowing . . . .
And I couldn't tie a ribbon around it
                even if I wanted to.

Ask something of me . . .
          please.
I know there is no answer . . .
          but often,
I need to feel it would be me
          you would ask . . .
if there was one.

I am not locking you out!
I am trying very hard
        not to lock you in!
Maybe it's, the same thing

What you seek is my approval . . .
        not my self.
So, it is more friendly
        that I turn you
        back to your self . . .
        the source
        of acceptance.
When you no longer need
        my approval . . .
I can give it to you.

You say you love me
　　　　because I understand you
　　　　better than you understand
　　　　　　　　　yourself.

Sometimes, like now,
　　　　I wish I didn't
　　　　because it forces me to see
　　　　that it is also the reason
　　　　you will have to
　　　　　　　　leave me.

You slept on your own side of the bed
                last night . . . .
It was a universe wide.
When I reached out to touch you
                all I could feel
                was the distance
                between.
It is still there today.
Your eyes . . . that soft bed of blue . . .
                once my resting place . . .
are crowded with distant mountains
                and racing rivers.
And I'll be alone . . .
                with you. . .
                again tonight.

This is no carnival!
I can ride with you . . .
but,
I am not
your
merry-go-round.
When you have discovered
the difference . . .
I'll meet you at the Ferris wheel.

I don't smoke . . .

so . . .

I never thought
I would miss the stale smell
of your bent,
charred cigarettes
on my bedside table.

But,

the clean ashtray
was as glaring
as a headlight,
last night.

I couldn't sleep.

If I smoked . . .

maybe I wouldn't have noticed
you were gone.

Maybe.

Let me be angry . . .
        please.
    It is the only way
I can keep you from seeing
        how much
        I need you.

If I say "no" to you
I will lose you.
If I say "yes" . . .
I will lose myself.
Even if I win, I lose.
Or do I?

I am not a piece of jewelry
to be worn
so that others will admire you.
If you choose to continue . . .
you must also remember
that when jewelry is displayed
. . . it can be stolen.

Will you try . . . just once,
        to be my age?
I'm tired of
        trying to be yours.

Stand up.
Let go of my hand.
Maybe then . . .
        I can let go of yours.
        You first.

I know you heard me . . .
but were you listening?

Better stop it now,
        before smiles become tightropes
        for words that step . . .
        with measured coolness . . .
across mechanical lips into deaf ears.

Please get the hell out of my life . . .
        only . . .
        go softly . . .
        and don't let me see you go . . .
or I may call you back . . .
        and there is no one home.

Wait!
You can't leave me now.
What will I do with all these
Oreo cookies?

I warn you . . . I will not die of you.

I warn you . . . I will not die of you.

The silence is so loud,
	I cannot hear my own advice.

Love, love . . . where are you?
You alone soothe the ache . . .
and I cannot believe in you.

Today . . .
I know how lonely I am
        for you.
I have mistakenly called
        four people
        by your name.

The most I can hope for,
right now,
is to make it to tomorrow . . .
just once . . .
without listening
for the phone.

I made the bed today.
I almost thought I was over you
. . . for a minute.

I never lied to you.
I always told you the truth
about love.

The joke is:
You listened to me.
I didn't.

CHAPTER THREE

I crowed
What I knowed
Bestowed
What I knowed
You hoed
What I knowed
And growed
What I knowed
But I slowed
What I knowed
And stowed
What I knowed
Then you goed
Up the road
And I blowed
What I knowed.

I know myself . . .
Now that you have left . . .
        I shall be everywhere
            hoping to make such memories
                with someone else.
That is when I will really feel
            you have gone.

My body is suspended . . .
My mind is lost in space . . .
My tongue just wobbles loosely
                    back and forth . . .
Saying nothing . . .
Doing nothing . . .
Out of time and out of place.
Like a bird . . . in dead of winter . . .
                    flying north.

What were you . . . ?
Who were you . . . ?
Something in me . . . I know that.
        But you were like a drug.
While you were near,
        you were the ultimate "high."
With you . . . I could split atoms,
        stop time . . .
        stay young . . . .
Or I thought I could.
But you only gave out small doses of yourself,
        enough to keep me coming back.
And I could never be sure
        when you would be available again.
Soooo . . . the inevitable crash . . . withdrawal!
I won't break windows, kill,
        or steal for a "fix" . . .
but I sometimes feel I might die
        for need of you.

As with tennis . . .
    never play "Love"
    with someone
    whose game
is not as good as yours.
You'll end up losing . . .
    and they won't
    know enough
    to care.

Without ever having you . . .
 I have lost you.
Without ever knowing you . . .
 I know you . . .
There is no history . . .
 Only a memory
 that never occurred at all.
 A memory . . .
 I can never forget.

It was a certain kind of sun, then . . .
And dreams and hopes hung like thick smoke
                    in the air.
Lyrics of songs jumped out at me
                like playful kittens around
                            a corner.
It is a long-remembered, half-forgotten time.
Where is it now?
Waiting for me . . . or for you . . . somewhere?
Or has it gone its way . . .
                    like the morning of your smile?

We weren't living together, anyway.
We were hiding together.

"Pain and loneliness make you strong . . ."
    I dish that one out a lot!
Today, I don't want to be strong.
    I want to dream just as much
    as anybody else.
But, I keep on paying my dues, anyway,
        and I really don't want
                to belong
                to that club
                    anymore.

You were so busy finding yourself
in me . . .
That I had to run from you
To keep you from killing
both of us.

Have you learned yet,
That who you know
    is not
    who you are?

The softer I walk
The louder I hear.

To own anything
        is to be owned by it.
I never wanted to own you . . . .
        It's impossible . . . .
And I never wanted to be owned.
But, I guess
        I always wanted you
        to pretend
        that you thought
        I was worth owning.

If all the "ifs" and "maybes,"
"wish-I-weres" and
        "could-have-beens-
        if-only-things-
        were-different-
        than-they-are"
could fall right off a cliff . . .
maybe I'd discover how
        to live with
        what is here and now . . .
but then,
I might as well forget this
        'cause I started it
              with "if."

In those moments of despair . . .
    when I really don't care
    whether or not I survive,
then, am I most keenly aware
    of the certainty that I will.
        That's the pain of it . . .
        and the miracle.

CHAPTER FOUR

I am astounded
        at how long it takes
                to discover . . .
        for the first time,
the things I have learned . . .
        over and over again
                all my life.

The real growth
is in recognizing
that we *do*
always get
what we want in life . . .
one way or another.

$\underline{N}$obody's perfect!
    $\underline{Somebody}$ doesn't have to be.

Most loneliness
        is pain . . .
peering into mirrors
        of self-pity
        with the hope
        of seeing someone else
                to blame it on.

Listen to what you criticize
                most severely
And you will hear
                what you most fear
                you are.

I was always afraid of
                risking *risk*.
But I found that I could stand
                to risk *risk*
better than I could stand
                to fear *fear*.
At least, risking
                brought about changes . . .
and the changes took up so much time,
I forgot what it was I was afraid
                to risk losing . . .
                in the first place.

The nicest thing about my life, now, is
that I am here with me
most of the time.

There is no such thing
            as perfect freedom . . .
There is only the freedom to
            discover
            that there is
no such thing
            as perfect freedom!

It is much easier to be lonely
            without someone . . .
than it is to be lonely
            with someone.

Real belief
     is a quiet thing . . .
     too busy being itself
     to look for disciples.

It is a waste of time and energy
        to worry about
                what others are thinking
                        about you.

        because . . .

You can never know
        exactly what another person
                is thinking . . . AND,
                the worst part is . . .
        they are usually not thinking
                about you at all.

They are too busy worrying about
        what others
                are thinking about them.

So, the truth is, all those terrible thoughts
        you thought they might
                be thinking about you,
        are your own thoughts
                about yourself.

Better spend your energy
          worrying about that . . . or,
              you just might
                  convince somebody to think
what you were afraid
          they might be thinking
                  after all.

It isn't always best
        to let everything
        spill out.
At times,
        there is more to be gained
        by using restraint!
Remember,
        it is the water
        held back by the dam
        that lights the city!

Always trying
            to be a good person
can be the biggest block
            to becoming one.

To live happily with a pet,
one must first accept
 the responsibility
 of disciplining it
 consistently and firmly
 with much love!
To live happily with ourselves . . .
 it is the same.

Who you are
  is not
  who you were . . .
It is who you are.

Any day of the week
I would choose to be "out"
    with others
    and in touch
    with myself . . .
than to be "in" with others
    and out of touch
    with myself.

I can tell how secure I am now.
I no longer clean the house
    the day before the maid comes!

Love is not a thing
        to be "in" or "out" of.
It just is.
The beginning is the ending . . .
and the ending . . . the beginning . . .
Always and
        never . . .
        forever.

In youth . . .
        man seems to satisfy loneliness
              with passion . . . .
And in maturity . . .
        aloneness . . . with compassion.
What a pity the difference
        is most often discovered
        after muscle and bone
        can no longer climb
              to the top
              of the mountain.

I have come to regard unrequited love
like a hole in a sock.
Mend it, or discard it!
Don't just stand there with cold feet!

Disciplining one's self
          can be carried
          too far.
It is alright to relax
          part of the time.
Even the soil is richer
          when it rests
          every seven years.

If I keep talking about
        what I believe in . . .
Eventually . . .
        I will tell myself
        how much I believe in
        what I talk about.

Since I've finally
        taken responsibility
        for my life—
I can't tell you how often
        I've wanted
        to give it back.

But, nobody wants it.

Isn't that lucky?

Nothing matters, now.
I mean . . .
          everything matters so much
that nothing matters now.

Alone can be beautiful.
It's the one truth
      we know to be certain.
      We are
      A Lone.
To embrace that truth
      is the first step
      to becoming
      Al One!

CHAPTER FIVE

I walk down another street.

Aware and alive
    to the little I know,
    as if I've arrived
    at another plateau.
    A plateau . . . familiar . . .
    yet,
    wonderfully strange
    where I find my milieu
    in the fortunes of change.

In my soul is a room
    with a wedding inside . . . .
    Alone
    is the groom
    and Truth is
    the bride.

Pity has gone
                    to its place on a shelf . . .
                    to be summoned for others
                    but
                    rarely for self.
                              Touching and feeling
                              in heart and in brain
                              Accepting the healing
                              of joy
                              that's in pain . . . .

Where *Alone* is not gloom,
                    nor a fearsome divide.
                              Alone is the groom
                              and Truth is
                              the bride.

Your alone-ness
          nourishes and protects
                my own.
I am always on the watch
          for you.
No need to wear a carnation!
I'll know you . . . by me . . .
          but you can hurry
          if you want to.